Underwater City

University of Central Florida Contemporary Poetry Series

University Press of Florida / State University System

Florida A&M University, Tallahassee

Florida Atlantic University, Boca Raton

Florida Gulf Coast University, Ft. Myers

Florida International University, Miami

Florida State University, Tallahassee

University of Central Florida, Orlando

University of Florida, Gainesville

University of North Florida, Jacksonville

University of South Florida, Tampa

University of West Florida, Pensacola

University Press of Florida
Gainesville
Tallahassee
Tampa
Boca Raton
Pensacola
Orlando
Miami
Jacksonville
Ft. Myers

Kelle Groom

Underwater City

Frontispiece and paperback cover photo: *Bayscape #3*, 2003, 15" x 20"
Ilfochrome pinhole image, popcorn tin pinhole camera.
Copyright by Marian Roth.

LIBRARY OF CONGRESS CATALOGING-IN-PUBLICATION DATA
Groom, Kelle.
Underwater city / Kelle Groom.
p. cm.—(University of Central Florida contemporary poetry series)
ISBN 0-8130-2751-9 (cloth: alk. paper)—ISBN 0-8130-2752-7 (pbk. alk paper)
I. Title. II. Contemporary poetry series (Orlando, Fla.)
PS3607.R64U54 2004
811'.6—dc22   2004041943

The University Press of Florida is the scholarly publishing agency for
the State University System of Florida, comprising Florida A&M University,
Florida Atlantic University, Florida Gulf Coast University, Florida International
University, Florida State University, University of Central Florida, University
of Florida, University of North Florida, University of South Florida, and
University of West Florida.

University Press of Florida
15 Northwest 15th Street
Gainesville, FL 32611-2079
http://www.upf.com

in memory of
Thomas Edward Smith
Edith and John Halunen

for Donna and Michael Groom
and
for Michael Burkard

Contents

~ part II

Acknowledgments

I am grateful to the editors of the following publications, in which these poems first appeared:

Agni: "Runaway Queen"
Chiron Review: "Leialoha—Valley of the Temples, 1970"
The Florida Review: "The Night Sky"; "Burial"
Flyway: A Literary Review: "Civil War Battlefield—Olustee, Florida"
Hawaii Review: "Bat Poem"
Heliotrope: "Rain"
Iris: "Woman under the Washington Street Church, 1853"
Luna: "Pinhole Camera"; "Home to an Island"; "Butterfly Dream"
The New Yorker: "The Boy with His Mother Inside Him"
Phoebe: "Underwater City"
Pilgrimage: "Two Black Suitcases"
The Southeast Review: "Drowning, 1983"; "Order for the Burial of a
    Child—Methodist Hymnal"
Witness: "A Syllable Missed Could Keep You at Sea"; "Pool"

My gratitude to the Money for Women/Barbara Deming Memorial Fund, Inc. and to the Atlantic Center for the Arts for support that provided invaluable writing time.

Many thanks to Judith Hemschemeyer, Russ Kesler, and Marian Roth.

Special thanks to my soul sister, Terry Ann Thaxton, to Michael Burkard for all his light, Lynn and Jerry Schiffhorst, Laura Palma (1961–2002)—beautiful painter who loved to hear every new poem, Lola Haskins, my teachers, Mark Doty, Kelly Cherry, Janean Williams and Dylan Rosales, Bethany Bower and Noel Haynes, Virginia Backaitis, Laurel McNear, Shareé Blais Thompson, Adele Azar-Rucquoi, Charlene, and my dear family for having faith. All thanks to Cory. Love to John, Jessie, and Julie.

though the earth tried to hold each one of them upright,
saying don't imagine don't imagine
there has been another like you—
—Brenda Hillman, "Small Spaces"

Who knows, for all the distance, but I am as good as looking
at you now, for all you cannot see me?
—Walt Whitman, "Crossing Brooklyn Ferry"

part 1

Pinhole Camera

I have to go to sleep so I can have my night.
The moon naked on one side, and Mars asleep on the other,

bright. In motion. There is a train & a cavern. Though sometimes
I'm so tired, the night goes to Tennessee.

I had told Iva, when the war is over, I'll come to Split.
See Tito's house. On the street she said she felt like theater.

We found a dark garden. She was trying to pick a rose for me. This one?
This one? She's thinking I don't find them beautiful enough. I don't like

their dying—last burst in my hand. She cried so much at the airport
that a man materialized underneath her chair, sound asleep
    on the carpet.

In between semesters, broke, I slept days, awake all night watching Carl
Sagan videos, reading books grabbed from library stacks—I knew

the librarians found me suspect, the way I'd wipe out a whole section,
photography, the Holocaust. So lonely, I almost bought a can

of Deep Woods Off to remember the scent of a boyfriend, but it was
too expensive (& poison). Considered spraying it in the drugstore aisle.

One night I opened Roman Vishniac's photos. The cover photograph of
a little girl in an underground room, a basement where her father
    had painted

flowers on the wall. Vishniac breaking into the ghetto with a hidden
camera. I'd heard about a camera woman on the Cape & her pinhole

camera. Her van is a camera, a karamel korn box can be a camera.
The van so big it took a long time to fill with light. Curtained, parked

outside a house, photographing it by taking all the light it can, until
an image of the house enters the van.

Carl said we are made of nails & water, coal. But that the opposite is not
true—nails & water won't make a person. He said we can't be reduced

to 90 cents. While explaining, he put nails in an aquarium & stirred.
He seemed to speak from the flight deck of a spaceship. In the midst

of the video marathon, I read in the paper that Carl had survived
a fatal anemia, his sister's bone marrow a perfect match.

For days, he'd been my only company. I had fallen a little in love
with him, his thoughtful explanations, his flared pants that made me

think he could dance. I watched the Mars video. Up close, the red
was sucked out—Mars looked dry, unpleasantly cold. An anteater-like

robot tilted in & out of ruts, pulling upright like a Weeble Wobble.
The film cut to Antarctica when Carl said that engraved on this robot

were the names of those who built it, that one man had died.
A glacier filled the right of the screen, blue sky to the left,

when Carl said Wolf Vishniac had done research in Antarctica because
it was Mars-like—but he had fallen off a glacier. A flash in my chest,

Roman Vishniac's dedication to *A Vanished World*, two names,
in memory, I find them both behind the girl's flower walls, flower eyes—

his father & also his son.
I found Werner Von Braun in a photograph—Hitler's missile man
    smiling

in Bavaria at 33. Broken arm like snow under his coat, saying
he is a nominal Nazi. (When I turned 33, an Argentine student said

you're the same age as Jesus.) Carl said Von Braun helped put a man
on the moon. He and his missiles in White Sands
    (V-2s that killed 2,500

Londoners, civilians). There was another book of photographs,
all the people of a little town, all taken in the Holocaust—the photo

album taken too. One girl, Lilli, was taken to a second camp,
most of her people had died, & she was ill, in the infirmary, war

almost done, the Nazis gone, & she needed a blanket, a towel, opened
a cabinet door, & under an S.S. man's pajama top there was an album,

all the people from her town, the album had followed her, found her.
She went to Israel, & years later, to Florida, & one day
   showed the photos

to someone who printed this book, & a copy found its way
   to my library.
I took it home. It has a rough brown cover, cloth, sack dress.
   In one photo,

the town's people are standing on a hill, grass, the wind is moving
through their clothes, their hair.

Pool

It was almost midnight in the laundry room.
The pool outside was turquoise, lit with underwater lamps.
My neighbors were violent drinkers:

a woman was often flung against the wall we shared.
My apartment overlooked the pool; the path to my door
was a narrow balcony, like a motel.

The neighbor man would try to bar my way, inviting me in
for a drink, and I would make excuses.
He showed up at the restaurant where I worked,

making conversation. One morning
I found a knife, a used condom,
and a pair of pants outside my door.

I used to leave the laundry room during the wash cycle,
but once or twice my clothes smelled like chlorine,
and I was paranoid that my neighbors

had dunked my clothes in the pool as a kind of joke revenge.
So, even though it was late, I sat in the laundry room,
read a paperback. Lovebugs and mosquitoes

fizzled in the blue bug light outside.
A stranger came in, navy haircut, bike shorts, no laundry.
He stood between me and the spinning dryer.

He said, *Can I ask you a question as a woman?*
If you were married and you had a fight,
and you left,

and something happened,
would you know you were loved?
His wife's car wrecked leaving him or coming back.

~~~

I didn't answer him even when he cried,
willing to withhold forgiveness,
a meanness

until he was halfway out the door, giving up, I said *yes*,
anyone could see it,
I can see it now.

The Night Sky

Monarchs arrive in Mexico on the first of November, which the nation
traditionally celebrates as the Day of the Dead. Some say they are souls
returning to visit relatives, or the souls of children,
—*Star Tribune*, 1999

In Sierra Chincua, *palomas* means king of storms, wanderer, milkweed
butterfly, souls returning, each weighing less than a dime.
You make a place for them, *los queridos*, an altar for your dead—

Marlboros, beer, tequila, their favorite dish. Buy flowers like marigolds,
form a cross. Strew petals to the door, the front yard. Stay up all night,
the dead will find you.

On the day my son would have been fifteen, I waited near midnight
in an Ybor City lounge, drank volcanic coffee with a man
        who imitated love.
A family ate dinner in the bar, restaurant long closed—
        the place so crowded,

my knees bumped their chair backs. Their boy watched
        from the gulf in his father's shoulder;
his mother said, *your son's flirting*. The hem of my blue
dress crumpled between us. Margot, the Cuban piano player,
        swept all the men

at the bar into the Degas she once owned when she was rich
        and watched
the woman's tired arms every day, loving the ironing. I wanted to kneel
beside the boy whispering from the dark, give him the soft emptiness

between my shoulder and breast, curve of gratitude, rest. Like the man
        in Sierra Chincua
who protects a forest because it's the blanket for monarchs,
because the cutting of a single tree makes a hole in the night sky.

Marguerite

My aunt Marguerite bathed three times a day
because her nerves were burning shingles.
As a girl, she had beautiful waist-length hair.
Everyone loved her sister.
When her sister died, she knocked on her stone,
twice, as if it were a door.

~~~

At the opera, an elderly man mistook me
for Faust's Marguerite,
blond, with small lines
like papercuts under her eyes. In prison
for murdering her child, she made a baby
of straw, rocked him. Mephistopheles flew in
from Houston with his three-year-old son,

who played the part of the baby.
Dressed in a white sheet, he comes from heaven
in the final trio. On the second night,
he got distracted waiting for his cue
by the curtain, came toward me,
a little sail, until the stage manager pulled him back.

When my son died
a thousand miles away,
I made my arms a cradle.

~~~

The veil over our eyes is thin,
the dead visible like candles through gauze.
Our souls relax at night,
and they are everywhere in the dark—
on the paths in the fields, in the wind,
alongside the living
with small lamps, sometimes flowers,
a heart or wreath made of pine.

~~~

City of Shoes

1.
In the Civil War
half the Union Army
wore boots
sewn in this city—
A city of shoes
for two hundred years—
thousands of workers
(Rocky Marciano was one)

2.
Uncradled
your bones
fit in a shoebox
Fragile outline
blooming
in ultraviolet light
like a small lamp
in a yellow covered book,
lamp in the dark trees
belled like violins,
land tested
full of arrows—
too contaminated
for a bus station

3.
Armfuls of children
rush after you—
birds across my face
Driving south
blue map thinner, solvent
Snow careless—left behind,
buckling, seamed

When I Was the Moon

I was ironing
a silver
dress,
days before
my father
put the phone
book
in my hands
said *tear it*
when he saw
my hands
were tearing
at the air

He'd let
me walk
out the door
my dress
smooth and quiet
I wore it
once
on Halloween
when I
was the moon

The Girl in White Beads

At a concert in Gainesville, I sat in the front row
listening to African songs, pretending I was in a garden

in a dream, not this glassed-in room of tulip dancers,
beaded drums, tin bells on the inside of my wrists.

When he died the flowers were for him, & I pretended
not to be his mother (*no one knows where he came from*),

I put my ticket away.
Everyone stood singing, & I was underground, shifting

like tectonic plates. Unable to stand songs anymore
not even on the radio, but the girl in white

beads sings to me.

On the Anniversary of Your Death

Car doors
were shutting,
loud frogs
on the pool
of water
between parking lots.
I lit
candles,
lots of them,
like the candles
I stared
into
as a kid
on the Cape,
the whole
church
in flames,
fainting.
I'd slip
down,
against
the hard wood.

Bridgewater

when i was 17 &
at bridgewater i had
a poster on my wall
from darkness on the edge
of town—my aunt
& uncle gave it
a funny look
when they visited, somehow
it seemed to indicate
my loneliness to them.

they had me visit —
we ate stuffed green peppers
& they offered me
a drink, kahlua &
milk, something
my parents would never do.

they invited me
to a family party—
i met the woman
who told me about
the suicide
prevention class.

two years later
they adopted my baby.
he died there,
& i remembered how it felt so gray.

while i stayed
with them i was
alone one day
outside—some outlet
store the only building
nearby,
lots of trees &
nothing, but not a good
quiet/emptiness, i felt
something not right
about it ecologically—
but then it just seemed
like something drab.

Easter

I wrote with my left hand,
in crayon,
to find out what I wanted:
read, *Why don't you go to him?*

~~~

On a bus near midnight
between Boston and the Cape,
nearing Brockton, I was afraid
to get off in an unfamiliar graveyard.

His toys are somewhere in this city.
I have photos of him, smiling,
dying at Easter, a basket on his lap

and one of him sleeping
in my uncle's shoulder, across his chest,
with red lines drawn
on his head by the doctor

~~~

Before he was born
I bought two blue receiving blankets,
kept them folded in a drawer.
On the fourth day, I gave them away.

I would like to hold them now,
wear them, sew them into myself,
I'm afraid that soon I'll have a small shovel,
sometimes I see my hands
reaching down.

~~~

Home to an Island

He was in the cupboard when the soldiers came. At night, I check my back door to be sure it's locked, & I think of the boy's mother, just murdered, moving around inside him, as she moved in their house at night, before sleeping, to be sure all the doors were locked. When I turn the handle, & it stops at the lock, in the turning I feel her traveling inside him. How can she leave him! & his knowing he has to release her, a boy. I remember my son inside me at night. How did he leave? I hope I let him go, that I released him. The light of the stars—you said the ones that don't twinkle are planets, Mars high in front of us. You said that we're part of the Milky Way, thirty percent inside, we can be in it & still see it. The moon kept rising when we walked away. I heard it was orange even here in Florida where he was born. Years after he died his adoptive parents drove hours to a tiny airport where I'd flown when my grandfather died. I came out of the little tunnel, little hall, & they stood at the end. I was surprised to see them until they looked for my son in my face. We visited before you came to me at the harbor wall. I saw their dogs, went to a restaurant. I ate a salad I think or fish, all the time wanting to say, please tell me a game he liked to play, his favorite game, a color, the sound of his voice. In the story, the boy in the cupboard ran & hid in a bog, until a man found him, covered him with his coat, took him home to an island.

Order for the Burial of a Child—Methodist Hymnal

for Tommy

I drive slow down rows and rows
In the Brockton cemetery,
Looking for trees, a family name.
After seventeen years I find my son.

When the people are assembled, the Minister shall say,
Lie down.
Bind us to the unseen world the dear and holy dead.
Fill your change purse with dirt from the grave.
Bury your silver fish ring with the turquoise eyes.

But trees loom up from nowhere and I can't stop
Gouging my eyes with sky, trying to stand on dandelion legs.
Bind us to the unseen world the dear and holy dead.
Plant your tulips in a hill of dirt,
The Minister shall say,
A cloud of yellow witnesses.

Lord, we have not any light to the place where he is gone.
I touch his stone name, the gates of heaven here somewhere
A secret paneled door.
Bind us to the unseen world the dear and holy dead.
Say it's Mom,
The psalm you knew,
The Minister shall say.
Fall open like a deepening sky, he'll rest in your blue arms.

Two Black Suitcases

I wanted to find Thomas Greenough, my relative—he was one of the
  few Wampanoags on Cape Cod who survived smallpox, genocide.
  After King Philip's War, there were only about four hundred left.

I miss the picture Nana showed me, Thomas, standing very straight,
  the photo disappearing. Or maybe it was his son, John.

After the war, a lot of Wampanoags dispersed.
  Some joined the Cherokees.

The colonists cut off King Philip's hands, sent them to different cities,
  Massosoit's son. Massasoit is the name of a community college. The
  colonists said they sold his son and wife into slavery in the West
  Indies, but some people think they got away, joined another tribe.

Thomas was the last surviving Indian in South Yarmouth, his relatives
  buried beside Bass River, and when the salt works were built, the
  town dug up their bones and buried them again on Indian Memorial
  Drive—I know it isn't a pile of shells and bones, piled high up into
  the trees, but that's what I remember.

In the Wellfleet Historical Museum, a guide told me they used to have
  the bones of the last Wampanoag woman in the museum, but now
  there is a note instead—it gave me the impression that her bones
  were tired of being on display, that they had buried her to give her
  a rest.

There's an island off Wellfleet, the path over sometimes under water,
  and when I'm there, alone, the light is so familiar and soft, it's like
  a voice.

I sent letters to people, asking if they could help me find Thomas—he
  had to give up his land after everyone else died, Indians couldn't own
  land, and one person wasn't enough for a reservation, so he moved
  to a pond.

He was a teacher.

The pond still has his name, it's called Greenough's Pond. As if you could call it, and it would come to you.

~~~

While I'd been waiting to pay my car repair bill, the mechanic had showed me a photo of the Hangar in Roswell where the government had kept an alien for testing—he said they cut the alien into pieces and sent parts to all the big companies, like GE, and after that he said, technology boomed.

He told me the most secret place is Groom Lake.

I was interested since it's my name and wondered what the government could do on a lake, I mean, how can you work on top of water, aren't you limited to the shores, like Thomas Greenough?

They say Thomas lived on a pond, but you know he was on the edge of it, and all the other Wampanoags in South Yarmouth—they lived on Bass River, but you know what that means.

It turns out Groom Lake was a lake when North America was covered with water, when we were one big ocean, the mechanic said, but it's a dry lake now, not even a basin, which makes it sound like you could drive right by and not even see it, except for all the security fence.

I looked for Thomas Greenough on Martha's Vineyard because there is a Wampanoag community there. Wamsutta (Frank B. James) was a Wampanoag who recognized Thanksgiving as a National Day of Mourning—he died in 2001.

In 1970, on Thanksgiving, he was supposed to talk at Plymouth Rock but the planners didn't like his speech, they suppressed it, said they would write it for him. Wamsutta said no, and for thirty years, he went to Plymouth and mourned his ancestors and the theft of their lands.

He said that when the Pilgrims arrived, within four days, they found baskets of corn and beans and took them, not recognizing that the

~~~

baskets were gifts to the dead, on burial ground. The government is willing to recognize some Wampanoags—the people on Martha's Vineyard, but not those in Mashpee.

I went to Mashpee.

It's hard to find anything there, everything seems quiet and unmarked. Finally, I went to a real estate office and asked, "Where is the Wampanoag burial ground?"

The agent was cheery, but unsure, she said there was a church with a graveyard, and pointed me down the road.

The cemetery was big, and I went around reading the stones—there were tall stones for founders or ministers, the church locked, but I looked in the windows, quiet, resting.

In a far corner of the cemetery was a big tree and a gravestone—bright cloths were draped in the tree and on the stone was a crown of branches and feathers, someone had made a circle of stones and a recent fire—I felt like I had walked behind a curtain into a secret place that was really the bright, open world.

As if I were the curtain I had gone behind.

This was the cemetery for Wampanoags, but I knew there was another one and drove around, looking for a person to ask.

When I saw a man, I pulled onto a shell drive. He said there were a few gravestones down the road, and a Wampanoag restaurant.

I drove past the stones three times—they were right on the road, in front of houses—it was getting dark when I saw their whiteness, maybe the dark helped me find them.

I stood with them for a while.

The restaurant was up on a hill, on a curve, a circle in. There were lots of framed photographs of Wampanoags on the walls. I didn't know what to say.

It was dark inside, dark wood, there was a counter and a kitchen and
seating in a room to the right, lots of people behind the counter, and
I didn't know what to say, I'm looking for a man who's been dead
for two hundred years, maybe I asked for a cup of coffee—I've been
away from Massachusetts so long, away from home, it's hard to know
what to say.

Canaan

The mother of all destructions was a fire
of 1,300 degrees, about twice as hot as a regular fire,
an explosion of flaming olive oil jars, timber walls and wind.

Ten miles north of the Sea of Galilee, it got so hot
that mud turned into glass,
and a stone library disappeared in the sand.

Lisa's house was an orange-groved refuge
from the Jerusalem winter of our Pontiac, my mother driving
the bumpy brick road, sure it would wreck the transmission,

on the way to my first junior-high party.
My goodbye sounded like eggshells—red slipped
in my wrists.

In the living room, Lisa looked through the sliding glass door
at the dark trees that were each a boy and a girl pressed together.
She said, *Go ahead, even you can find someone.*

Burning in my white sundress, white sandals that clicked
when I walked (I couldn't walk);
then in the glass I saw the dark a boy could touch.

Opals

In the black lake
I swam out to him,
waiting to be lifted,

to wrap my legs
around his waist, water
falling from my lips,

his fingers
touched the stones
at my throat.

On the shore,
our skin damp,
we dressed in our jeans

and turned to the dirt
road where the others were,
their voices ran up

along the side of the lake
waiting to be found—
he turned,

no words,
just his hands
circling my neck,

into the leaves
and the wet
grass

he moved me
down, a blue
shadow, bones.

~~~

Drowning, 1983

In a cement duplex
On the Fourth of July,
The doorknob hid a secret lock,
Or alcohol slowed her wrist.
Drinking undermined her,
As the sea undermines a tower
Steadied by ropes,
And men climb to remove the lens and beacon.

She was strangled by men
Who pounded her as if between
Two stones.
Drowning without water,
Dunes or winding sheets
Of seaweed,
Grabbing ocean sand for sky.

The struggle was more
Than the struggle
To be born
And still not enough.
When time stopped,
There was a sort of breathing
Without breathing,
The body not hers,
Finally sweet, a girl,
Full with her parents' sadness.

2

Some angel put his mouth to hers—
A radar echo
As from birds or rain—
Carried her blue shadow,
Dressed her in one murderer's jeans (over his complaint),

A vial of fake cocaine in the pocket
Like a coin,
Set her down on the Sunday morning highway,
Dust kicking up inside her shoes.

3
No crowd at the harbor, fireworks expired, drifting
Like talcum on the sea.
Almost home by night,
Wet hair quilted with blood
She heard her name called twice.

He looked like one of the earliest angels,
Who had no wings and were like men.
So careful, they would lift you up
In their hands
So that you would not strike your foot
Against a stone.

Colonial Mall I

An old woman
came in
slow
and asked
where the old
girls were—
I told
her none
were working
that day,
and she said,
"Tell them
my husband,
the one
with two
canes, died."

Colonial Mall II

A girl was wheeled fast through the mall,
she was lying flat on a high bed,
and her face was sideways

toward the window of my store.
A small and roundish woman pushed.
The girl's face was wild,

mouth stuck with fear,
her eyes pulling
everything she saw inside.

Her hair didn't fit on the bed,
it fell off the end,
so long I wondered how

it didn't catch in the wheels,
her hair flying as the bed
drove by.

The round woman didn't seem
big enough to be pushing that fast,
the bed seemed to go on itself,

then, the wild Rapunzel girl
saw me
and she pulled me inside.

Rest of Loves

Sand dust in my eyes, the light in Honolulu stripping lady
palms down skinny rills.
When you were drunk, I drove the Catalina on the pitch dark road,
your wrists bent in crucifix strings, blond hair
covering your face like a skylight.

The moon full blue, calling your name all night to be sure,
my hand on your chest, I could feel the heartbeat
on the left side of the rib cage (rest of loves)
because the bottom left corner of the heart tilts
forward, comes closest to the sewn face of the body.

Wake

in memory of Peter Homer

The family sitting with the body all night, in Old English, it's "wacan,"
to *arise*, in Sanskrit, it's "vaga," *strength, speed*. The space in between
full of waves, then a long hall like a tunnel. After twenty-five years,

Janey, whose father has died, says, *I'd know you anywhere.*
She took me horseback riding, and I held onto her waist,
my arms around her like a belt,

but Janey remembers the stars my mother gave me.
Her face on someone's shoulder, broken open, and I wish
I had gold stars for her long hair, something shining.

The freckles on my right leg match the stars in Orion's Belt—
the bright ones between Taurus and Lepus—and when I see them
in the night sky, it feels familiar, like my body magnified.

On a topographical map I've seen Ancient Cemetery
where my relatives are buried, where there is a spot
bought for me, the river

where my ancestors lived a thousand years, the two-bedroom
cottage on Bass River where Dad's lung collapsed
from raking pine needles (he's allergic to pine), the Red House

on Follins Pond, the White House in South Dennis,
the treehouse in Dennisport, Mimi's house (my sweet collie),
the Vietnam party at Nana's by the Red Cottage Store,

the Homers' front yard
in summer, and Young Peter saying, *You always live in warm places,*
like a kind wish.

At Home, after Cards

beyond the dunes
the vines are ripe
the bog a red sea
past your knees

so go to your wife
as she's falling asleep
and by heart
stroke her hair

until she feels you
like a fire in the room,
untie the line now
cross over

Burial

for E.I. Halunen

Pitchpine, woodbine, hemlock,
bayberry sweeten the briny air.
At your husband's grave
you step, unaware,
outside our hymn
and reach out
for the next minor tune
of humming consolation,
the next hand,
but are left saying oh,
the word unraveling
until we,
like black branches
in a relentless wind,
rush in.

At night
your daughter
smoothes the counterpane,
touches your sleeping face
while you walk back
on the wet sand
fifty years
to the first house on stilts
near the marsh and the rough grass
drenched by the dark scar
of his shade,
his thirst for your salt.

Four Clocks

In the back seat of the car, sticks leaned together
like the bones of my relatives

taken from their grave near Bass River
when the salt works were built,

and buried beneath a stone on Indian Memorial Drive.
They died from smallpox, long fevers,

burning up before they went into the river.
In 1797, Thomas Greenough, my great-grandfather times four,

was the last surviving native on the reservation
in Mattacheese, "Indian Town," so settlers took the land,

and he lived on a pond
that from the air looks like the body's heart: two ventricles, an atria,

a curve like the entrance to a cave—now it's a Boy Scout Camp,
named Greenough's Pond.

My grandmother showed him to me in South Yarmouth,
a photograph that disappeared in the room

with a glass jar of pennies on the bureau
after she got so tired of being sick

and asked that her ashes
be thrown into Bass River.

When she died,
I spoke to her in the old church

with four clocks
where time can be seen from all directions.

Leialoha—Valley of the Temples, 1970

Rained all night. Blue Angels flew over early. Hot, but a good breeze. Byodo-In Temple,
Windward Coast. Had to cover our shoes before we went in. Rang the five foot tall
gong—it sure made you vibrate. Mountains behind us. Just beautiful.
—Edie I. Halunen, travel diary entry

On the temple's red bridge, I won't let go of her,
we hula like coconut shells,
    ten thousand carp, graveyard flowers,
I have her blue flight bag,
she counts thirty-one planes from midnight to seven.

We hula like coconut shells, ten thousand carp.
Graveyard flowers—pink for leis, plumeria;
her heart exhausted.
From here we can see the Blue Angels' show
    over Kaneoke Bay.
She counts thirty-one planes from midnight to seven.
They float down light as butterflies, a necklace of

plumeria, leis, her heart exhausted.
I have her blue flight bag,
the face of her grandmother
on the temple's red bridge.

Late As It Is

When eleven days were removed from September, 1752,
the English cried, *Give us back the days you have robbed.*
Scientists say in the last fifty years, one second has been lost,
an unspent second saved like the birth of Christ in the ring
of a sequoia.

I saved your Mother's Ring, a stone for every child—
sapphire, ruby, amethyst, aquamarine—your nightgowns saved
from charity, sailed like wedding dresses over my head, like sleep—
when I wore them, my wrists ached
with something sharp and intravenous.

You saved a handmade wish I'd sent 30 years ago—
Hurry opin this card . . .
(My orange clock read 10 o'clock, inside another read 11),
I'm as late as it is, but Happy Berthday in magic marker green,
a green hand Vulcan salute.

Late before I could even spell, you died while I was in the air
or asking after lost bags, or waiting on them, clothes.
Three days to choose a coffin to burn, urn to bury, obituary.
Time is the difference between before and after,
the day come and everyone gone.
When I put my head on your chest, you sighed—
my kiss left a mark, a red blur
like your mark on me.

One night before supper, you took me to the marsh,
said, *This is my favorite place.*
In the summer dark, I hit a ball down the long dirt road,
an incandescent second—ran tree, tree, T-shirt, home.

Later, we forgot the popcorn popper top,
as the kernels heat, they bombard us—
you're laughing so hard, you're crying,

popcorn raining down on us, the counters, chairs, linoleum,
corners, kitchen sink,
we're helpless in each other's arms,
there is no way to stop it.

Wedding

She had a little apartment with a buzzer
in case she fell, like she did the winter
after he died, her foot slipping on the icy snow,
falling down the hill that swelled
from the street to her front door.

Alone, two ribs broken, she picked
herself up, drove to the hospital.
Then she sold the house, got the apartment
with the special buzzer.
The heart attack was on my birthday—

I was in a cabin in the woods, phoneless,
eating cake when her heart stopped, and she hit
the buzzer on the wall.
A week later, I came home and found a card
from her, a hundred dollars, birthday wishes,

love—my father called that night to tell me
about the surgery, how she'd wanted to die
because no one told her that the tube in her throat
wasn't forever.
When they sent her home, her legs swelled up,

she couldn't walk, nurses came on a schedule
to dress her, feed her.
On her birthday, I sent her a ring
with a blue stone
to marry her to me,
clear as the water that meets the marsh.

Runaway Queen

At night, I imagined her in the funeral home,
   groggy in a twilight sleep,
putting up with the inconvenience, the orange and white dress,
going too long without food, time running out,

like in the dream I had about my son when I gave him away:
he was just born, and I kept him inside a record album.
After three days I remembered he'd need food and ran to find him,

sleeping and alive. I was surprised at my grandmother's request
for a cremation, hoping she didn't really want her body,
the way she'd wanted to keep the house, but never told us

until the end, too late. I thought she was breathing
when I held her in the coffin, afraid she'd be burned alive.
Years later, a woman befriended me, Pauline. She gave me

a personality test, and the night she graded it, ran to me in a gold
ball gown, like a runaway queen, to say I'm Joan of Arc, *because
you know how she turned out.*

I finally told Aunt Diane that my grandmother had breathed.
Diane said doctors had done all the tests. One of us stood
   on the staircase,
the other on the landing, talking up and down.

Diane said the body can hold on to breath when nothing's left.
That's why when everyone had gone, and I held on to her,
she sighed.

Letter

Edith Irene Halunen, d. 1998

In "A Letter to Three Wives," a man in love stands with a reluctant,
poor woman in a kitchen while a train goes by,
and it shakes him so hard, he almost falls down, pans crashing,

he's nervous too, and the train shaking the kitchen rattles him
until he's almost in pieces,
but the woman just hangs on and smokes a cigarette.

The train going by my apartment shakes me on the couch, in bed,
like the driver's trying to wake me from a dream, the trembling
coming from inside, the way ground carries the sound of arrival.

You would have liked the restaurant we chose, good fish,
candle light. At the next table, there was a woman
with your face, I thought you'd come back somehow,

then the woman was a stranger again,
and I stood in the parking lot next to a sky blue car,
my hands flying, turning over and back,

like a woman showing off a manicure or a wedding ring.
I know you flew to your son, you hadn't seen him alive
since you zipped him up to go sledding,

husband to find, your mother, grandmother dead
before you were born, Sarah, who gave me her face and hands
so she could touch you—at night the train conductor calls so loud

he wakes me up. Can you hear it there?
How did you find time to come to the restaurant,
to put your arm around me in the black car?

The Atomic Dance

When I glance away from the window
a dark bird falls from the sky

(as if diving from the roof)
& I catch him in the corner of my eye.

When you died
they shocked you back,

too late
to say goodbye,

electricity & metal
on your sweet tired heart

your gown.

Ocean Ring

I'm not good at giving gifts.
At first, I bought the ring for myself.
It seemed when women wore rings
they were loved.
No boyfriend ever bought me a ring.
No "promise ring" in high school.
Twice engaged to be married,
still no rings.
The first time, I was eighteen years old.
He gave me an "engagement watch"
with fake diamonds, cubic zirconium.

~~~

When I realized I could buy rings for myself,
I didn't know anything about stones.
At the antique store, I would choose pretty
rings—fifteen or twenty dollars each.
The ring I bought for myself, then gave to Nana,
was a blue oval with mother-of-pearl circling it.
Silvery petals.
It reminded me of the ocean.

~~~

Nana loved to give gifts.
She sat by my bed on a schoolday
in Massachusetts, my parents working,
my throat sore. She was laughing.
Her happiness made her seem in motion,
like a bell.
She gave me orange sherbet and 7-UP
in a tall glass, Bradlees' bag
with a new board game.
Cold out. Her hand on my forehead.
She worked part-time at Irwin's Pharmacy
just for the extra money, for gifts.

~~~

~~~

I taped the ring in an envelope,
with her birthday card—or maybe I just set it in.
It stuck out a little, made the envelope bumpy.
No box, no wrapping?
I had the idea of marrying her to me,
wedding her to earth.
I was anxious to get the ring on her finger.
She'd been very sick.
In the hospital, they had wanted to put a tube
in her throat. She said she'd rather die.
She was tired of needles, punctures.
I wouldn't want a hole in my throat, a tube.
But she'd have sat beside me for that too, like
when I had four wisdom teeth pulled and woke
with my tongue worrying bloody holes unpleasantly gauzed
(the gauze sticking
to my tongue), woke up crying,
and she was there. Though my mother told me
we were living in Hawaii or Florida then,
that she was thousands of miles away.

~~~

My mother and my aunt were in the hospital
with Nana. In 1965, my aunt's brother
had given Nana's youngest son a push,
pushed his sled down a hill. A kid is always
grateful for a good push. The sled hit a tree,
and he died. Seven years old.
My aunt is the one who convinced Nana
not to die. She accepted the tube and lived
and then lived for awhile with my aunt,
recuperating.
Nana told my aunt, *You're not getting this ring
when I die.* Maybe my gift came in the mail
while she was living with her.
It seems there was some upsetting conversation
going on and this became a part of it.

~~~

Nana understood the ring was precious.
Royal.

~~~

I helped her into bed once, pulled the sheets up.
Her legs were beautiful, like a young girl's.
We had two sharpnesses when I was a child:
my not knowing how to shape a hamburger patty,
and not knowing where to place the zip code on an
envelope. The practical things I could do
were limited. She knew I loved her enough
to take care of her, knew I didn't know how
to take care.
It was mostly how she looked at me,
saying I was like I had always been,
and this was said/shown with unmistakable love
for my undomestic hands, leaving her
in the practical hands of others.
Years later, very few, she died unexpectedly.
There'd been a scare, but she was feeling better.
My aunt told her I was coming. Then her heart
stopped, and the doctor brought her back.
She died again, and he let her go.

~~~

In her bedroom, all her rings were in a drawer,
including the one I'd given her. I packed up
her sheets, two pairs of slippers, nightgowns,
her quilt, the clothes she'd wanted to donate
to the Cancer Society Thrift Shop—
and mailed them to myself.
Her sweaters. At home, in Florida,
I would take out a sweater (she wore the white
ones more) and smell her in the wrists, collar,
the perfume points.

~~~

The rings in her drawer: Mother's Ring, a stone
for every child; engagement ring with worn-

~~~

down gold, soap from washing dishes
still on the back of the band, caught behind
her finger. The gold in back thin as a wire.
Gold wedding ring. I took everything,
scooped it all up before my aunt's family arrived.
I did show my mother, trying to get a feel
for my behavior, my taking.
I felt Nana say, *Yes.*
My mother sort of looked at my hand
holding the rings. I think she nodded.
My aunt did arrive, looked for the rings.
Or maybe I just had to show her.
She mentioned someone unmarried.
Her daughters? Me?
That they should have the wedding ring. I think
she said it kindly.

~~~

I wanted everything Nana had touched—coffee
mug, blue flight bag, Tic Tacs. My aunt did wind
up with some rings (though years later,
she gave me every single one). I knew
my mother would want the Mother's Ring,
so I kept it, protected it for her, so when
her sadness lightened some, the ring wouldn't be
lost to a relative, like photos in a basement
that you have to ask permission to see. As if
the basement owns them.

~~~

I kept the engagement ring, soap and diamond
and worn gold, wearing it even once might break
the band, so I keep it in her white evening purse,
in her flight bag. It fits on my smallest finger.
Some nights, when I'm afraid or nervous,
standing guard at the opera for instance,
I wear the ocean ring, bring her along.

~~~

White Butterfly

the white butterflies came to me the spring and summer she died. in cocoa beach, i'd turn on i dream of jeannie lane to lori wilson park, where one night i saw two peacocks wandering in front of the nature center's closed doors, the male a walking galaxy, and days the white butterflies would be all around the path to the beach & trees.

i couldn't work or anything for missing her—i could float in the ocean, move little, stay close to where she'd stopped in this world—i was listening, & the white butterflies flew all around.

the first time, i was so surprised to find her in a butterfly—i'd come home from shopping, paper bags in both arms, up the little hill to my door, hoskins holler, & i saw her flying for me to see,

how she landed on the grass of the little hill, & i slid down too, my bags still in my arms & sat with her for a long time.

so long a neighbor across the street yelled, are you all right? thinking i had fallen. i thought *can't you see she's here with me, she's here.*

Kukla

Sometimes I think when I was suffocated & died,
I lost much of my childhood memory.

I'm just jotting this down so I don't forget.
When you read the Amichai poem with two girls

who overflow & vanish, I had the feeling
from Kukla, Fran, & Ollie movies—

the European ones: children in a field, rain,
my heart beating fast.

During the war, I stood on my bed
at the top of the house,

arms upraised & screamed,
the tongue of a bell calling you home.

Civil War Battlefield—Olustee, Florida

"30,000 flee walls of flames."
—*Orlando Sentinel*, July 2, 1998

After Neal's wedding
in a field
dizzy with cake and sun and strangers,
we left Tallahassee.
It was the day the fires began.
One roadblock after another,
I-95 closed,
a dozen houses gone up,
a salvage yard.
We took smoky back roads,
brave in your new truck,
headlights on,
and found a Civil War battleground in Duval County
burning down around us.
In the thick air was a little rain,
the last for weeks.
Cannons pointed at us.
Three thousand men were dying here
in 1864.
Stranded, swaying grass.
I took you in
my bare arms,
swirls of burned pine
floated,
my arms burned,
the bare pine took you in.
White ash like thick snowflakes
in our hair—
you'd never seen the real thing
even in Ithaca at seventeen,
you were gone before winter;

on your packing list
Evelyn wrote her name at the bottom.
It *was sweet*, you said,
having left her long ago.

Underwater City

He walked into the lake
as if it were grass,
to float a second in its light,
disappear,
be a place.
The cypress trees up to their knees in water,
coiled ladders
reading the necklace of his DNA.
      High sky, a canoe
figuring the circumference,
underneath the hull
wavery with smudges, musicians' black coats.

~~~

Black cautionary tale of eighth grade:
another boy
shooting up, withdrawing
his vein with the needle,
      tugging it out—
a magician's red scarves.

~~~

He talked to the dark like an orchestra pit,
      ceiling of black net,
light below:
            an underwater city,
a place to steady down the trains,
the constant passing by,
the pots of coffee drunk, something winglike
panicking inside.
      I waited for his hand,
the tight instruction of his thumb,
invisible birds on his lips—
      fluttering, a blur like sleep,
      water swimming away.

~~~

The Speed of Everything

Black birds in trees
Attacking the girl with red hair
Claws in her scalp
Wings beating in my ears
Red bird in the battlefield
Blue bird in backyard
Diving in front of windshields
Having to break for them
Protect them
Thinking they understand the speed
Of everything, wind, cars,
But not in April/May
Bird in the grill
Of a neighbor's car
Like a toy, orange plastic beak
Red wing fanned out,
Red in the hair,
Eyes half-closed and gone so gray
Afraid to disentangle
How you fit between the bars
& strangled, one wing free, your face,
Little crown of feathers
So close & calm, stopped in a wild
Turn, it feels that we could almost speak
To each other

The Boy at the Copy Shop

the boy at the copy shop, white shirt, smelled of warm laundry,
girl in the library of love's baby soft—
   that smell of fifteen-year-old alive
in satellite beach florida, & spraying it on for free at the eckerds
across from the red bridge that connects to the navy base, past
the red satellite high, never saying yeah scorpions, spraying
the pink alcohol fizz behind my ears, on both wrists, inside my
warm elbows, down my shirt if no drugstore people were looking,
the ocean and the feel of the air with boys in it, smoking
on a tailgate, quiet, watching you,

he's in a k-mart in south carolina & smelling vanilla, a big thick candle,
   a year of vanilla,
he's buying it, unlikely purchase, but it smelled of me,
vanilla melting on his door of a desk, under the lamp,

my legs here, vanilla,

every time i cook in the oven he gave me when he left, the old
spills burn, smoke, and every time the air conditioner has to be
put on high to avoid the smoke alarm—its alert circle of red,
to avert flying out of the house again at 4:30 in the morning
with my hair half-wet in my last clean pair of underwear,
& an old pink robe my mom gave me, nana saying

you won't even need a towel after your shower, your robe's so thick &
warm, or was it mom who i need now more more more, saying
we went to dean's for nana's boxes, but there was no tea set from italy
for you, it's gone, a mystery, how it helps to see someone else
loving her gone to the bone, in the bones,

i burned my finger in the oven, melting cheese on the potato,
protein, so i won't sleep all the livelong day, the woman on the
radio saying she felt better with eggs in the morning. it was hotter
than it looked. red & burning, a tiny fire in the cells.

Woman under the Washington Street Church, 1853

She was buried under glass, almost floating the churchyard.
One winter Sherman said, *Lie down to sleep, safe in my hands*

as if wholly your own, then burnt the town, the church
beside her. The new church bricked her underneath,

like war china in bedsheets—the only way in was a hole
in the broom closet floor. The woman's story was passed

down to me, heard at a party—someone hadn't wanted to let
her go, buried her under a window. I lived in a cabin behind

a stained-glass store, then in a treehouse, on the beach,
in a dark, low house in the snow. It was already dark when

I found her church and climbed over air-conditioning pipes
the size of small cows, over the wire playground fence,

pushed open the gate to the oldest cemetery, grass lumpy
like bodies under my feet, dirt cantilevered, as if it would give

way, send me cascading into a sinkhole of the long-dead,
their bumpy limbs. In daylight, the janitor would probably

let me in, but I'm afraid of the broom closet shutting,
like the oval plate over her face, a lid, a hand over my mouth,

afraid of the crooked house my bones will make alone.
In the dark,

one of her eyes has slipped open a little, indigo-rich—
night pond swimming inside—

though she's gone, passed through her skin like a winnowing
house, through the page of her dress, through the sieve

of church walls, through methodist song,
through salt print and press, and the bleakness of ink,

pouring out of his hands black from the fires
she's passed through.

Butterfly Dream

I was riding in back, legs stretched out
on the seat, my supervisor driving. Al, a co-worker, up front.
We're driving by a lake. My supervisor says fog rolls in,
& every five days or so they find a body in the lake.

He is matter-of-fact about this, & I look away, out my left
window & see thousands of white butterflies flying straight
toward me, my open window. I smile & close my eyes.
I know it will be big, letting them all in the car.

It is as if they'd come once before.
There is a calm, dark woosh, like going under a wave;
then, the butterflies are settling down on my stomach & hips,
womb, my *hara* below my belly button (which a healer

once said to cover while sleeping, to protect against bad spirits).
The butterflies are damp, like white flowers in Hawaiian
leis, petals fallen with the cool inside on my skin, layers
& layers of those petals, so many that I'm afraid to move, afraid

of the car's movement, that one will be crushed.
Some of the ones on top look a little dry, brownish—
are they thirsty? They were so quiet, at first I worried
they might be dead. But I remembered butterflies are quiet

when they sleep. The men in front have no butterflies.
Al says, *What is that on her?* My supervisor says, *It's butterfly
dew.* Al understood it as butterfly *ee-euh*, something
disgusting. Maybe the butterflies made love on my body?

I felt they wanted to heal me, like a laying of hands.
The more the men in front talked, the more the butterflies disappeared.
But I could feel the weight of them, the dampness of their wings,
damp joy, white kiss, thousands of them, covering me

with wishes, heaven flutter.
Years ago, I knew two sisters, twins, both beautiful
with long dark hair. One went to my school, she rode a bike,
but sometimes she'd ask me for a ride. She was studying a difficult

language, Japanese I think—a different alphabet. At first I felt
a little jealous of her beauty,
& I was selfish about helping others & nervous with acquaintances
(in particular in my car), but the sister was very steady/calm,

& it began to seem a privilege to have her in the car.
She told me she had been abused, her sister too. Her father did it.
& I could not imagine how a person would survive this,
how she would love a man, breathe. One day she told me

she'd asked her counselor if she could talk to her father &
her counselor said yes. I saw how much she loved him, how much
she wanted to see his face, the abuse a blackness her love shone on.
She was a little girl in my car. Near the end of the semester,

we were driving up University Boulevard, maybe halfway
to her apartment when she told me a recent dream. She was looking
at the yellow shag carpet glued to the cracked dash of my car,
not at me, saying, *I just opened my legs & hundreds of butterflies flew out.*

Water House

Dr. David Pendergast of the Royal Ontario Museum
was sent to Cuba to supervise the tourism of the island's

archaeological sites. Wooden statues had been found
floating in the water. He dammed a bit of lagoon

with sandbags & plastic sheeting, sucked the water out,
dug in the muck & found more wood, posts, then thatch.

A woman in the audience gasped when he said *thatch*.
It meant something to an archaeologist. The house was whole,

a circle house. They left it because you can't dig a house out
in three weeks with water seeping in under the sandbags.

The next year, they dammed another spot, & found another
house, square. Beams fell together, a slanted house.

When people live in a house, thatch can last forty years,
you have to patch in places, but it will last.

If the people leave, the empty house will lose its thatch
in three years. Just fall apart, disintegrate. *It's a mystery*,

he said, *but true*. Finding thatch was a miracle, the Indians gone
four hundred years—everyone believing the Spanish

killed them off in the seventeenth century. But the Indians hid,
protected by the deep woods, now a plain, & mountains & were

blocked from ship's sight by keys. *Now in Cuba*, he said,
you'd have a hard time finding enough wood to build this lectern.

Their houses lasted because they were water
houses built on posts. In the warm dark of the auditorium,

I remember almost reaching Lieutenant's Island, though
the tide would have come, washed the way back. But it was time

to meet the boat, hot & sunburned, out of bottled water.
Salt water soaked shirt around my head. Purple bikini top

meant for a lover long gone, my chest burning. Not knowing
what a hike required. Climbing over the rocks on the near island

to swim in the bay, cool off, before rushing back.
No fort in sight, just a sign. The marsh grass holds

the light my grandmother loved. I would shake it out, carry it to her.
Open my palms, & she would tell me the story

of her first house on stilts, near the marsh & the rough
grass, & the pond nearby where the children go.

She would tell me I am not a ghost
in my life, that I did not die with her, did not fly

out the window
into darkness, hidden by the deep woods, now a plain.

and when I couldn't count
it counted,
that bright love counted me—
—Brenda Hillman, "Spare World"

part II

The Boy with His Mother Inside Him

You said meet me by the harbor church, tide wall, little beach,
and while I waited I walked into the water, salt in the flare

of my jeans. A light went on in the house next door,
a stranger was farther down the shore, no moon, ocean quiet

with me waiting. When I stood, I felt the darkness of the tar,
and then the darkness of the night, and then you were behind the turn

of my head, behind my one Heidi-ponytail, behind my green
corduroy jacket, the night like a big hat on my head

turned with me to see you.

How Does Your Soul Find the Glass?

Who is the architect for building careless of the door's window, past
    warehouses, cemetery, Dunkin' Donuts, rain chair?
Who got left behind rating quality of life in surrounding cities—
    leather solvent spilled on the ground, in the water?
Who said he knew TCE from the office grave, between sheets
    in *Boston Magazine*?
Who said "contaminated"?
Who said TCE from the tannery—that's copy machine cleaner?
Who married an architect?
Where is elliptical west?
Who floats red flowers, taught by a Japanese man, down the hill
    of a new world?
Who stares for all you care?
Who is not there?
Where is the black soil, the rumpus room, the leaves with oilcloth?
When the greenest trees went by, why had their formation been trees
    so long?
Who is from another school, tamped down?
Who kissed for luck?
Where are the kids in Woburn of the drowned?
Who was in Brockton two years leaning on his seat back?
Who veiled the mouths of sixty factories?
Who from the 1700s was alone night after night when my father said:
    a dark-haired boy?
Who has a study room alongside common icy hair?
How does the salt run free and skylight?

~~~

Address

Are you here right now?

Why was I able to see you in the bathroom mirror at Dave's house
after he left to build the Grand Prix Raceway?

Why did you appear after I'd been crying for my grandfather,
with my face in his rocking chair, touching the brown fabric
he had touched?

You said that you'd been with me always, would always stay—
where were we before this?

Does it bother you that so often I see my skin and think it's me?

Does it bother you that I forget to look for you?

That I'm afraid to look for you?

Are you so beautiful because your fear is gone, like the woman
who suffered from a disease that destroyed her amygdala,
the almond in the brain where human fear comes from?

You look just like the person I meant to be—
when I saw you, was I in there too?

I told my friend about you, after she told me that God
sang her three songs:
(1) Nat King Cole's "Unforgettable" after her mother died
from Alzheimer's,
(2) Joe Cocker's "You Are So Beautiful" at the Aretha
concert, and
(3) The Platters' "Only You" on the car radio.

Why do I worry that people will think my friend is a
fundamentalist? She isn't somebody who would
come knocking on doors—she's very reserved, a nurse.

The week after our talk, my friend said she had something
to show me in the trunk of her car. It was a mirror
she'd bought at an art show years ago—there were Scrabble
letters in an arc at the mirror top and bottom. The letters said,
"The face I now see is not the real me."

People on TV

That night I dreamed I had just come to live with him,
but there was another woman in the house. He had asked her to stay.

She was heavy and dark. Her body and her clothes. All day she watched
TV, ate, slept. All our conversations were sitcom discussions,
    plot synopsis.

I locked myself in a room to get away from her. She was a wedge
between us. We were living on $180 a month. Her mouth crammed

full of food, glistening, bubbles of saliva at the corners of her lips.
She was eating all the food. I recognized her when I woke up.

She'd been with me three years ago when I refused to come back
from my grandmother's death, all I wanted was to hide and sleep,

the only people I saw were people on TV. She was a wedge
between myself and life. Nothing but time ever made her leave.

~~~

Not Sylvia Plath

I had a dream that I went to a university like yours,
brick and stone, pounded on the doors,
but was locked out.

I dreamed of a woman I'd never met before,
an artist and a writer who'd lost belief in her talent.
She'd done sea drawings,
like your swirling prayers in the dune shack,
kneeling in a green cloak.

Your office at school is an alcove, a nave.
The window has a castle arch, looks out on snow,
a square of sunlight.
I sent you a photo of myself at nine in Honolulu:
tablet on my lap, pencil held up,
one wrist shy and bent almost to hide the whole operation
in the carport shade.

Someone came into your office, asked, who is the girl
in the picture?
You told them I was Sylvia Plath.
Later you said, "It could be anyone."

I found the ocean behind a cliff of sand.
It looked like the beginning of the world,
no people or buildings,
no one to save me
when I went underneath the water, and it let me in.

A Syllable Missed Could Keep You at Sea

A syllable: when he went jogging, sometimes he'd pick up sticks
to save them from being run over by cars.

He'd put the sticks in his pockets and return them to the woods,
or sometimes he brought the sticks home.

Missed: once he took a stone from Green Lakes, a tiny fossil inside,
but it felt wrong, and he tried to return it to exactly the same place.

Could keep you: when Bethany would see a motorcyclist on the road,
she'd always get behind the bike, to keep the other cars

from crowding. At sea: when my father went to Vietnam, I learned
how to hurt myself to keep another safe. It had to do with repetition.

Bat Poem

At night in the swamp, his girlfriend was tagging bats
the first week they met—endangered eastern big-eared bat,
body like a thumb, wingspan of a couple hands, medieval face,
rabbit ears. She'd catch them in mist nets, weigh & tag fast,

no more than twenty minutes disentangling—a bat could die
from the stress. She'd had three sets of rabies shots (bats bite),
though if you blow gently in their faces—(she blew gently like
this, like a kiss, like the uselessly gentle hair dryers in Italy)—

it startles them, they stop biting. She told me the bats' scientific
name, Cory, my brother's name, *Corynorhinus rafinesquii macrotis*—
they need a special kind of tree that's been mostly mowed down.
One winter my brother said he & his wife didn't have fun anymore.

I asked him when was it fun? *Like in Boston,* he said, the time
she saw a TV show bar, laughed, made him stop the car, *Let me out,
I want to run in & pee in the bathroom in Cheers.* He tried to drive
around the block, but the road led to a highway, & he was gone
    a long time.

Helplessly

My father arrived an hour after I'd caught
my foot on the futon, broken the third bone
of my toe ("little piggy" the medical tech said)

like a wishbone pulled wide, purple at the snap.
At the clinic, my father lent me his arm,
so he waited in the doctor's office with me.

He raised his eyebrows at a textbook on the counter—
instructions for taking X-rays—we laughed
so helplessly, I had to lay my head down on my knees.

When the X-rays came back, the doctor showed them
to my father, as if I were a little girl.
It had been years since the day I gave my father

a ride to work, and he'd leaned in to kiss me goodbye.
We were not a kissing family—my grandmother
was the only one who'd ever kissed me on the mouth,

Coral Moon Drops kisses, but only because her love
was wide and without aim.
When my father kissed me, it was as if we'd both

forgotten who we were. I was drinking then, out nights.
One morning I came home with cigarette
lighter burns along the insides of my arms, my car

smashed into a truck stopped at the light,
Southern Comfort an orange spill down my white dress.
My father didn't have a second car then, had to bike

down the highway to see the damage.
Or maybe that particular accident came later,
and it was the girl in me he'd kissed goodbye that day.

~~~

The Promise of Anesthesia

This poem reminds me of when I was in labor with my second child,
   and I turned my face to the wall, preferring the darkness of death,
   but I was called back by the promise of anesthesia.
The poem left me perplexed.
These are my fave lines.
You can come up with a better line.
A possible cliché if you will.
Who slept on this?
This is not an ending. It doesn't resolve anything.
Very homey.
Why does the narrator want to wake up? Isn't sleep the next thing to
   do at this time?
Goats don't have arms!
Obviously she has been there before, or has experience
   with farm animals.
Can you eliminate the gerunds?
Yeah! Such a warm feeling here.
I would make a definite transition here to the past.
   (I feel certain about this.)
This says, "Hey, look at me, I'm poetic."
Smoldering.
This is a good sentence.
Incomplete sentence.
Is this a story or just random thoughts?
I must be dense. What was her crime? I've read this four times and still
   don't know. Is it slapping the baby?
Anterior past uses past perfect tense.
You have some nice phrases; I underlined them—
Your writing has an element of vagueness. More detail and description
   may fill in the blanks!
Interesting sing-song.
Blood and berries are a good mix.
What is metaphor and what is reality?

B's story of wanting to die, feeling like this during childbirth, made me
    think of migraine headaches. I don't think I want to have kids if
    they're anything like a migraine. I know this doesn't relate to your
    poem. I'm just chatting.
Trim. (Cut these four lines and I'll be happy.)

Another goat—this must be the semester for farm animals.
I want more of a feeling of why.
Bursting should do something more active.
I don't get it. Gingivitis brought on by grief?
Did you make up that word?
I wish I could be more helpful with poetry, but I haven't studied it yet.
I've been proofreading Disney's Guide for the Hearing Impaired and
    this forced reading of the lyrics to "It's a Small World," "Pirates
    of the Caribbean," etc., has caused the poetry-reading portion
    of my brain to flee, screaming, into hiding.
I find it hard to critique poetry because of its form.
I'm looking for a tinge more emotionalism.
Definitely doesn't fall under the common rhythm of poetry.
You might could tone down the abstract imagery.
Some really nice images of cliffs, the salt, and a fin. The fin
    was a definite tip-off for me.
Interesting use of a word with biological implication.
Sensory details: 10.0   Flow of syntax: 7.5
This makes us suck for air—we're not supposed to have
    that feeling here.
Reminds me of the 33rd St. jail the night of my DUI.
Sentences were real long.

This House

you scratch an image on glass
make a photographic print
press
      the pale yellow oil
      of cloves
glue organza to the soft ground
pour ink so stiff
      it breaks off the mixing knife
      like butter
rosin dust sparks
in a closed box
acacia gum, chalk, gesso
      fill your porous bones
so we can hold your carbon arc, lamp & tissue, damp lacquer
      your eyes'
            thirty-five colors
                of charcoal & pastel
      the bevel of your light

Girl in the Blue Dress

All night the saw palmetto fronds, netted chain, willow weed,
swish dark against the cypress walk, cabin, wind,
he paints the girl in the blue dress, holding sunflowers, tired
in the hot sharp light, her shoulders slumped, eyes bloodshot
Every night in the cabin, painting the same picture—blue dress,
hair pulled back, hands crossed on her thigh

Distortion frightens her, her arms painted too long, or that story
he's telling about eating mouthfuls of alizarin crimson,
squeezing the paint tube, turpentine burn staining his mouth
for days, vomiting red suicide
She thinks of men who swallow swords, eat ground glass,
spit fire, that old freak show of pain

She'd like to wash his palette clean of color, fix coffee,
teach him to swim, garden, he brushes alizarin into her hair,
as if he's spelling syllables, in paint her skin a hieroglyph,
her shimmering of human light dresses bone, flames star-bright,
shearing walls of cedar, glass

Illegal Aliens in Spain

letter from my mother

In the Guest House in Madrid
Dad left his dancing shoes under the bed
It was my fault he said
I was supposed to look.

So Dad bought a pair of short boots
Because there weren't any shoes that looked like boots.
Dad's never been able to wear boots
With that "leprosy" on his shin.

He was saying in his loudest voice,
Seventy-five dollars for these?
I asked Dad to be quiet
But he said he wouldn't.

I don't have much news. We are always busy.
Can you do those disco dances?
Kids do them on breaks at square dance class,
Dad can do most of them.

He tries to teach me,
But I'm not a fast learner,
Cory just laughs at Dad.
The car is being cleaned at the garage,

Underneath it is covered with snails.
Did immigration give you trouble in Philly?
We were supposed to send your passport to Cadiz
To have the Valido stamp unvalidoed.

If it isn't unvalidoed,
You cannot leave Spain,
And you have to give them time to do it.
I went in plenty of time

Only to find
We were never given the Valido stamp.
We have been illegal aliens in Spain.
They used to not let you out

But they will
If you fly military.
Did you get in a big hassle in Philly?
We danced for three days and nights

In the Jamboree in Tivoli
And in a Spanish wedding.
Then we danced on the deck of the ship
To win a badge before the *Canopus* goes to sea,

It was so hot the records warped.
Tonight I'm in a quiet house,
Dad's on watch. Cory's racing in Zaragoza.
Guess I will read the night away.

Hours

You lost a lot of blood,
like when you fell at the lagoon,
the beach jungle gym,
hand over hand, and then you were broken,
the long hall, empty,
your faraway scream.

In South Carolina, your foot wouldn't stop bleeding,
couldn't make it stop.
The sliding glass broke when you went through it, headlong
from sleep, glass in your foot. Party guests still
in the house, babies asleep, your wife in Clearwater,

I forget her name in the panic:
it's Beth, Beth so angry said she'd take the kids, leave.
Four days in the hospital, operation,
a month off from work.

Yesterday you walked a mile on the treadmill.
I lived every day with you—all my life,
years and years in our little rooms,
next to each other
all over the world
when I sang every night for hours.

At the Oscars

It was twenty-eight degrees this morning, so I took Westmoreland,
the back way, didn't want to see three hundred
men in blankets standing on Vine
just past the giant red cross.

At work, a homeless blond girl,
two or three years old, was pushing a stroller so intently,
she didn't hear my questions.
From behind, a woman answered,
said the girl's name was K.

A family lives in the room behind my office, I can hear
their radio. Once I went behind my corridor to see
dozens of tiny, windowless rooms.
When one door opened, I couldn't breathe.

In the afternoon, I opened my door
and the girl was there, pushing her stroller down
the carpet. When I said, "It's Miss K!"
she looked amazed, as if her name had been called
at the Oscars. So pleased. I bent my knees, so we could see
each other easily, asked her doll's name.

An older woman came along, said, "That's her new
stroller." Brand new. That's why this morning
there was no sky or hello.
I told her we had the same name, and again her face
so open-mouthed astonished, as if I'd said that we were sister
astronauts, that we'd be flying to the moon this afternoon.
Miss Luminous.

When I Was a Bird

One night, feathers grew
in a cape,
wings on my legs.
I tried to show you,
but you wanted to tell me
some terrible news
about Afghanistan, and I said no,
you won't be able to hear
that the feathers are a gift,
the wings always here.
The cape heavier than you'd think,
feathers layered and dense,
like a thousand slices
of baklava.
The night before,
you dreamed I was circling
above you in a plane
that tried four times to land
but couldn't.
When you woke, I was still in the air,
and you read me
Katherine Mansfield's story
"When I Was a Bird"
from your Tall Book of Make-Believe.

Rain

i'm raining on your hair &
your neck, on your mouth
& your kiss, your hands, palm
lines, fingertips, on your
stomach, my hair
raining on your hips &
your thighs, all along your
back (you don't need the
swim trunks), along the arc
of each foot.

i'm raining on the back
road to my place, in all the
phone booths, little beach
with orange moon, at all
tables, raining on you
when you're with the
moon, the ocean, any stars,
in a lighthouse restaurant,
all meetings, when you
drink a cup of coffee,
raspberry/twig or burdock
tea, & when you're near
the sun, a yellow pantry, a
bed (white or blue), a trap
door or blinds, a pillow.

i'm raining on your secret
field, your secret road,
your house with the yellow
guitar, lying next to you, rain
falling all around.

Notes on the Text

"Pinhole Camera"
Lilli Jacob Meier's book of photographs is *The Auschwitz Album: A Book Based upon an Album Discovered by a Concentration Camp Survivor, Lilli Meier* (New York: Random House, 1981). The collection of photographs by Roman Vishniac is *A Vanished World* (New York; Farrar, Straus and Giroux, 1983). The "camera woman" in the poem is Marian Roth, who has received fellowships for her pinhole photography from the Guggenheim Foundation and the New England Foundation for the Arts.

"Home to an Island"
The story of the boy in the cupboard is from Anne Michael's extraordinary novel *Fugitive Pieces* (New York: Alfred A. Knopf, 1997).

"Two Black Suitcases"
The church in the poem, the Mashpee Old Indian Meeting House, was established in 1637. It is the oldest Indian church in the United States and the oldest house of worship on Cape Cod.

"Woman Under the Washington Street Church, 1853"
The woman buried under the Washington Street Church in Columbia, South Carolina, is Sophia Catherine Nance, who died on January 24, 1853, at the age of twenty-eight.

Kelle Groom's poems have appeared in *Agni*, *The Florida Review*, *Hawaii Review*, *Luna*, *The New Yorker*, *The Southeast Review*, *Witness*, and other journals. She has received three fellowships from the Atlantic Center for the Arts, a grant from the Money for Women/Barbara Deming Memorial Award Fund, and a writing residency from the Millay Colony. She has taught writing at the University of Central Florida, Seminole Community College, and Valencia Community College and is currently director of grants at the Coalition for the Homeless of Central Florida. A native of Massachusetts, she has lived in Hawaii, Spain, Texas, and most recently, Florida.

Photo by Michael H. Groom

Judith Minty, *Dancing the Fault*

David Posner, *The Sandpipers*

Nicholas Rinaldi, *We Have Lost Our Fathers*

CarolAnn Russell, *The Red Envelope*

Don Schofield, *Approximately Paradise*

Penelope Schott, *Penelope: The Story of the Half-Scalped Woman*

Robert Siegel, *In a Pig's Eye*

Edmund Skellings, *Face Value*

Edmund Skellings, *Heart Attacks*

Floyd Skloot, *Music Appreciation*

Ron Smith, *Running Again in Hollywood Cemetery*

Mark Smith-Soto, *Our Lives Are Rivers*

Susan Snively, *The Undertow*

Katherine Soniat, *Cracking Eggs*

Don Stap, *Letter at the End of Winter*

Joe Survant, *Rafting Rise*

Rawdon Tomlinson, *Deep Red*

Irene Willis, *They Tell Me You Danced*

Robley Wilson, *Everything Paid For*

John Woods, *Black Marigolds*